KNOW IT ALL!

ANIMALS

MOIRA BUTTERFIELD AND PAT JACOBS

Cavendish Square
New York

Published in 2016 by Cavendish Square Publishing, LLC
243 5th Avenue, Suite 136, New York, NY 10016

First Edition

Website: cavendishsq.com

This publication represents the opinions and views of the author based on his or her personal experience, knowledge, and research. The information in this book serves as a general guide only. The author and publisher have used their best efforts in preparing this book and disclaim liability rising directly or indirectly from the use and application of this book.

CPSIA Compliance Information: Batch #CW16CSQ

All websites were available and accurate when this book was sent to press.

Cataloging-in-Publication Data

Butterfield, Moira.
Animals / by Moira Butterfield and Pat Jacobs.
p. cm. — (Know it all)
Includes index.
ISBN 978-1-5026-0892-5 (hardcover) ISBN 978-1-5026-0890-1 (paperback) ISBN 978-1-5026-0893-2 (ebook)
1. Animals — Juvenile literature. I. Butterfield, Moira, 1960-. II. Title.
QL49.B88 2016
590—d23

Project managed and commissioned by Dynamo Limited
Consultants: Sally Morgan, Dr. Patricia Macnair, Brian Williams, Carey Scott, Dr. Mike Goldsmith.
Authors: Moira Butterfield and Pat Jacobs
Editor / Picture Researcher: Dynamo Limited
Design: Dynamo Limited

KEY – tl top left, tc top center, tr top right, cl center left, c center,
cr center right, bl bottom left, bc bottom center, br bottom right.
All photographs and illustrations in this book © Shutterstock except:
Corbis 27c Pallava Bagla, 27cl Karen Kasmauski; iStockphoto.com 18tr.

Printed in the United States of America

Table of Contents

Brilliant basics!

All About Animals

Animals live everywhere on Earth, in every type of climate and landscape. The study of animals is called zoology.

What is an animal?

How can you tell an animal from a plant? Here's how:

1. An animal has a body made up of lots of tiny cells that have a different structure (they are built differently) than plant cells.

2. An animal does not make food, as plants do. It eats food from elsewhere.

3. An animal can see, hear, and feel its surroundings because it has sense organs—parts of the body that give it senses such as touch. Different animals have different senses.

4. Animals have voluntary movement, which means they can choose to move their bodies.

Animal groups

Zoologists classify animals in groups with Latin names, from a big group down to a small group. The classification of a lion, shown below, is an example. A lion is in several animal groupings. The biggest group is at the top.

Kingdom – Animalia (animal)
Phylum – Chordata
Sub-phylum – Vertebrata (vertebrates)
Class – Mammal
Order – Carnivora
Family – Felidae (cat)
Genus – *Panthera* (big roaring cat)
Species – *Panthera Leo* (lion)

Types of animal

Here is a closer look at the animal groupings.

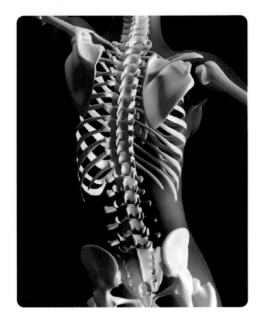

↑ Phyla

There are about thirty-five different phyla. One of the most important is Chordata, which includes all the animals with backbones (vertebrates). Invertebrate animals do not have a backbone. They make up many phyla including arthropods and mollusks.

↑ Classes

The best-known animal classes are insects (*above*), mammals, birds, fish, reptiles, and amphibians. Insects are the biggest class. There are several smaller classes too, such as anthozoans (sea anemones), gastropods (snails), and arachnids (spiders and scorpions).

↓ Families

Orders break down into animal families. For instance, Carnivora is broken down into Canidae (dogs), Felidae (cats), Ursidae (bears) and many more meat eaters.

↑ Orders

Orders are the next group down from classes. For instance, the orders in the Mammal class include Rodentia (mice and rats), Primates (monkeys), Carnivora (strictly meat-eating mammals), and lots more.

↑ Genus and species

Families are broken down into genus. For instance, the family of Felidae (cats) includes *Panthera* (lions and tigers) and *Felis* (domestic cats). The genus *Panthera* is broken down into species such as *Panthera leo* (lion) and *Panthera tigris* (tiger).

 Know it all!

● So far around 1.3 million animal species have been discovered and named.

● Swedish botanist (plant expert) Carolus Linnaeus invented the classification of animals, called taxonomy.

● Human beings are the *Homo sapiens* species, meaning "wise man" in Latin.

🐾 Food connections

All animals need to eat food to get the energy they use to grow and move. Some creatures eat plants. Other creatures hunt the plant eaters.

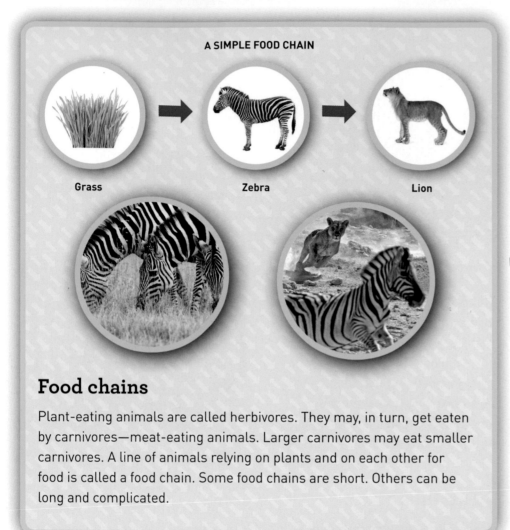

A SIMPLE FOOD CHAIN

Grass → Zebra → Lion

Wild elephants eat around 650 pounds (300 kilograms) of plant material every day.

Food chains

Plant-eating animals are called herbivores. They may, in turn, get eaten by carnivores—meat-eating animals. Larger carnivores may eat smaller carnivores. A line of animals relying on plants and on each other for food is called a food chain. Some food chains are short. Others can be long and complicated.

Eating for energy

When animals eat, food passes into their gut where it is broken down into smaller parts. It then passes into the blood and is transported around the body. When it reaches the cells, it is broken down further and energy is released. This energy is used for growth, to carry out repairs, and to move. Plant eaters have to eat a lot more food than meat eaters do because plants are difficult to digest.

Food webs

Most animals are part of more than one food chain. For instance, herbivores will usually eat more than one type of plant. Carnivores will eat more than one type of animal, and omnivores (such as humans) eat both plants and animals. The interconnected food chains in an area can be joined to make a food web. If one part of the web fails, for instance if a plant or an animal dies out, the rest of the web may find itself without enough food.

Hot shots!

★ FUSSY EATER

Giant pandas eat only one thing—bamboo. Because bamboo is very low in nutrition they must eat up to 84 pounds (38 kg) of it a day, which takes them around twelve hours.

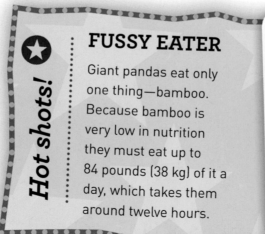

🐾 Animal habitats

The community of all the living organisms found in a particular place, together with all the nonliving parts, such as soil, is called an ecosystem.

River pollution can lead to the death of plants, fish, and then larger animals.

All about ecosystems

An ecosystem can be large, like a forest, or as small as a pond. The largest ecosystems, such as tropical rain forests, are also called biomes. A habitat is the place where an organism lives and finds its food. An ecosystem contains many different habitats, each with its own animals. Within a habitat, the living organisms depend on each other for food and are linked together in food webs.

One tree or pond can support lots of creatures, such as insects and birds, in its own habitat.

Ecosystem dangers

Human activity poses a major danger to an ecosystem if it damages the environment. For instance, pollution in a river may kill the plants that the fish eat, quickly leading to the death of the fish and then the death of all the animals that eat the fish. Ecosystems may also suffer if they become overcrowded with creatures that eat all the food and water available.

The biggest ecosystem

The biggest ecosystem on Earth is Amazonia, the vast rain forest that stretches around the Amazon River in South America. Zoologists estimate that many millions of different animal species live there. Many of them have not yet been discovered or named.

The Amazon rain forest is by far the world's biggest ecosystem.

💡 Know it all!

● One of the toughest habitats for animals is in the deep sea where it is always dark, and cold. The deepest-living fish found so far were spotted by a remote-controlled submarine 4.8 miles (7.7 kilometers) deep in the Pacific Ocean.

● Caves are also cold, dark and isolated habitats. Animals that live in deep cave systems tend to be blind and find their way around by feeling their surroundings.

Mammals

Mammals are a varied group of animals, from tiny bats to giant whales, living in all kinds of habitats around the world. Humans belong to the mammal group.

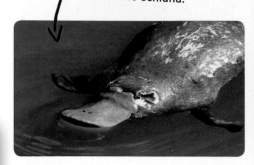

The duck-billed platypus is one of only two mammals that lay eggs. The other one is the echidna.

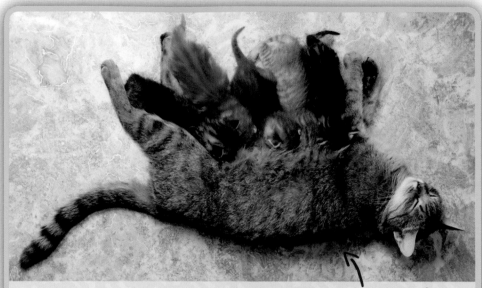

A female mammal produces milk to feed her babies.

What is a mammal?

● Mammals are endothermic (warm-blooded), which means they can keep their body temperature warm all the time.

● Female mammals suckle their young, feeding their babies with milk from their own body.

● All mammals have skulls and backbones.

Different types of mammal

There are three types of mammal. Placental mammals, such as humans, have babies that are born with well-developed bodies. Marsupial mammals, such as kangaroos, have babies that are tiny and less developed. A kangaroo baby is about the size of a peanut, and after birth it crawls into its mother's pouch, where it feeds and grows. A small group of mammals, the monotremes, lay eggs and hatch their young. The Australian duck-billed platypus is a monotreme mammal.

The cleverest mammals

Primates are the mammal group with the most complex brains. They include monkeys, lemurs, apes, and humans. Many primates have the ability to stand upright for long periods and have more highly developed hands than other mammals. Some primates can use their hands for complicated skills such as toolmaking.

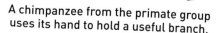

A chimpanzee from the primate group uses its hand to hold a useful branch.

💡 Know it all!

● Whales and dolphins are ocean-living mammals.

● The bumblebee bat from Thailand is one of the smallest mammals. It weighs around 0.07 ounces (2 grams).

● The blue whale, the biggest mammal and the biggest creature on Earth, gives birth to the biggest animal baby by far. A newborn whale calf can weigh up to 7.7 tons (7 tonnes).

Birds

Birds are endothermic animals with backbones, wings, and feathers, though not all birds can fly. They live all over the world.

Flying birds such as this zebra finch have extra-strong flight feathers on their wings that help to raise the bird in the air.

A COLORFUL CROWD

These pink flamingos are examples of wading birds with webbed feet to help them paddle. They get their pink color from the natural dye found in the shrimp and algae they eat.

Bird feathers

Bird feathers are waterproof, and they help to keep the bird warm. They are made from keratin, which is a material also found in hair. Down the middle of the feather there is a hollow, horny shaft called a quill. The flat part on either side, the vane, is made of tiny fibers called barbs, all locked tightly together by hooks to create a smooth surface.

The nest of an African weaver bird

A bird of prey such as this European eagle has a beak shaped for tearing prey.

A hummingbird using its slender beak to get nectar from inside a flower

Bird beaks

Birds have a horny beak to help them feed. Birds of prey (hunting birds) have sharply curved beaks for tearing their prey apart. Seed- and nut-eating birds such as finches have powerful beaks for cracking open their food. Fish-eating birds have long, sharp beaks for spearing their food, and nectar-feeding birds have long, slender beaks for reaching into flowers.

Eggs and nests

Birds breed at certain times of the year when they know there will be food available for their babies. Many birds build nests, where they lay their eggs and hatch their young. Nests vary in shape and size, depending on the bird. One of the most complicated is the bell-shaped nest of the weaver bird (*above*). It gets its name from the way it threads its nest together.

Reptiles

Reptiles are a group of animals that are ectothermic (cold-blooded) and have scaly, waterproof skin. Most lay eggs with tough shells. Lizards, snakes, crocodiles, and turtles are all reptiles.

Crocodiles and alligators

There are 120 species of crocodiles and alligators. You can tell the two apart by looking at the mouth and snout. When a crocodile's mouth is closed you can see its fourth tooth sticking out over its lower jaw. A crocodile's snout is long and narrow for catching fish. An alligator's snout is wider, making it better for crushing prey such as turtles.

Snakes and lizards have skin scales. This python's skin markings are created by its scale colors.

The biggest crocodile ever found was more than 20 feet (6 meters) long.

Snakes

Snakes are limbless reptiles, ranging from the tiny 4-inch-long (10 centimeter) threadsnake to the 23-foot-long (7-m) python and the giant anaconda, which weighs up to 330 pounds (150 kg). Some snakes have fangs that produce venom to kill their prey. Others kill their victims by coiling around them and constricting (squeezing) them to death.

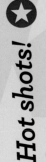

Hot shots!

★ TODAY I'M FEELING GREEN

Some lizards, such as this chameleon, change their skin shade depending on how they feel. They might want to show off their brightest skin color to attract a mate or to signal to their enemies that they are angry and ready for a fight. Other lizards will understand the color message.

Amphibians

Amphibians are a group of animals that live partly in water and partly on land. Frogs, toads, salamanders, and newts are all in this group. They have moist, slimy skin and breed in fresh water such as lakes and ponds.

Newts and salamanders

Newts and salamanders look like tiny lizards, but they do not have skin scales. Salamanders have smooth skin, and newts have rougher skin. They come in lots of colors, some very bright to warn predators that they can secrete (seep) poison. They spend their time hunting worms, insects, and snails.

Newts and salamanders live in or near water.

Frogs and toads

There are lots of different types of frogs and toads, including ones that burrow, climb, or even glide from tree to tree. Frogs have smooth skin and lay their eggs in clusters. Toads have rough, warty skin and lay their eggs in strands. Most toads have poison sacs behind their eyes, to make them taste nasty to predators.

Toads tend to be fatter and wider than frogs.

Changing babies

Most amphibian babies metamorphose, which means they change completely in shape to become an adult. For instance, frogs hatch as tadpoles from eggs laid underwater. Over a few weeks they gradually grow legs and turn into frogs that can breathe on land. The grown frogs hunt creatures such as insects and small fish.

HOW A TADPOLE BECOMES A FROG

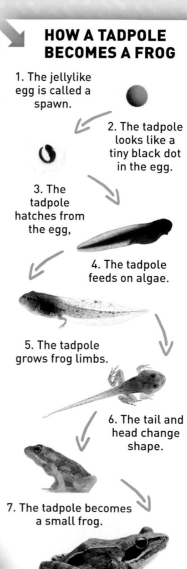

1. The jellylike egg is called a spawn.

2. The tadpole looks like a tiny black dot in the egg.

3. The tadpole hatches from the egg,

4. The tadpole feeds on algae.

5. The tadpole grows frog limbs.

6. The tail and head change shape.

7. The tadpole becomes a small frog.

8. The frog can live on land or underwater.

Fish

Fish live in ponds, rivers, lakes, and oceans. They are an ectothermic (cold-blooded) group of animals, so they cannot control their own body temperature.

Know it all!

● Most female fish lay thousands of tiny eggs that float in the water until they hatch.

● The female seahorse lays eggs into a pouch on the male's body. The eggs hatch there.

A fish's body

Most fish have these features:

A streamlined (smooth and curved) body shape for slipping easily through water.

A waterproof, scaly skin that stays moist. Eels and lampreys are the only fish with smooth skin.

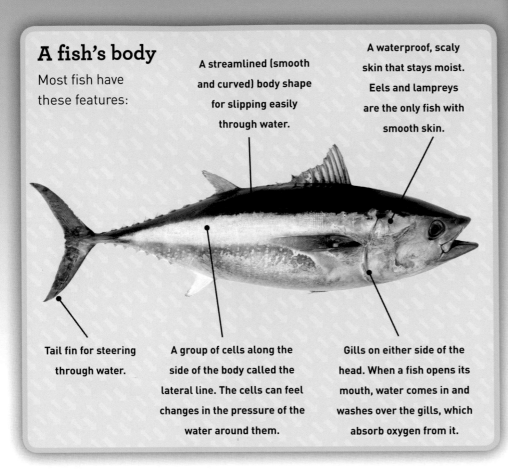

Tail fin for steering through water.

A group of cells along the side of the body called the lateral line. The cells can feel changes in the pressure of the water around them.

Gills on either side of the head. When a fish opens its mouth, water comes in and washes over the gills, which absorb oxygen from it.

A manta ray is an example of a cartilaginous fish, with gristly cartilage instead of bones.

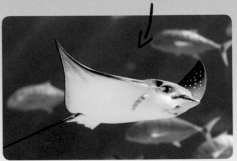

Bony or not?

Most fish have a bony skeleton and a little air-filled sac called a swim bladder inside their bodies. This bladder acts rather like a water wing, keeping the fish afloat. Cartilaginous fish are different. They have skeletons made of tough, gristly cartilage instead of bones, and they do not have swim bladders. This makes them heavier than water, and they sink to the seabed if they do not keep swimming. Sharks, rays, skates, and dogfish are in this group.

Different types of fish

Fish are a very varied-looking group, ranging from tiny, fingernail-sized dwarf goby fish to giant whale sharks 40 feet (12 m) long. Whale sharks are the biggest fish, but unlike many sharks they don't hunt other creatures. Instead a whale shark swims along with its giant mouth open, collecting tiny animals and plant material floating in the water.

A whale shark, though huge, is a gentle creature.

Insects

Insects are the biggest animal group on Earth. They are found all over the world, even in deserts and freezing regions where other creatures find it hard to survive.

Being an insect

Insects are ectothermic, and they do not have skeletons inside their bodies. Instead they have a protective outer covering called an exoskeleton. Their bodies have three main parts: a head, a thorax (middle section), and an abdomen (back section). They also have three pairs of legs. You can see these body parts clearly on a wasp. The head has the eyes, antennae, and feeding parts. The thorax carries legs and wings. The abdomen protects organs such as the heart and may carry a sting.

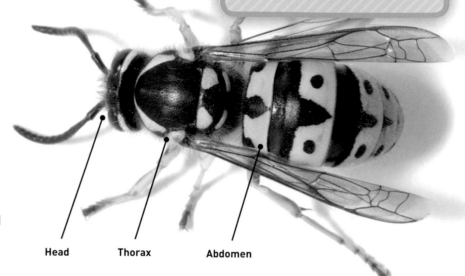

Head   Thorax   Abdomen

Know it all!

● Some butterflies have scented wings, to attract a mate.

● Some insects, such as lightning bugs, have lights on their bodies to attract mates.

Growing up

Insects go through metamorphosis, changing their body shape completely as they grow. This picture shows how a caterpillar changes into a butterfly.

HOW A CATERPILLAR BECOMES A BUTTERFLY

Larva   Pupa   Butterfly

1. A female insect lays tiny eggs, sometimes on the underside of a leaf.

2. The egg hatches into a larva. Caterpillars, grubs, and maggots are all insect larvae.

3. The larva grows, then changes into a pupa (or chrysalis) inside a hard case.

4. Inside the pupa the insect's body reforms in a new shape. Eventually the adult hatches.

On the insect menu

Some insects eat plants and nectar, while some hunt for other creatures. For instance, damselflies and dragonflies use their fearsome-looking mouthparts to catch other flying insects. A dragonfly will form a basket with its legs to scoop up an insect in flight, then quickly crush its prey in its powerful mandibles (jaw parts).

Crabs, Sponges, and Starfish

Crustaceans, echinoderms, and sponges are three animal groups found underwater, mainly in the world's oceans.

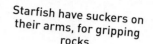

Starfish have suckers on their arms, for gripping rocks.

Crustaceans

Crustaceans are a group of more than forty thousand animal species, all with hard shell exoskeletons. Crabs (*below*), lobsters, and barnacles (*above*) are all in this group. Crustaceans have jointed legs, gills for breathing underwater, and antennae for sensing the world around them. They wave their antennae, testing out the taste and smell of their surroundings by picking up chemical molecules floating in the water or air.

Sponges

Sponges are a group of simple creatures that are anchored underwater. They are often found on coral reefs, where they look rather like plants. The body of a sponge is covered in tiny pores (holes) through which water flows. The sponge filters out tiny organisms from the water to use as food. Sponges grow in different sizes, colors, and shapes.

A sponge on a coral reef

Echinoderms

The echinoderm group lives in seawater and includes starfish (*above*), sea urchins, and sea cucumbers. They have an endoskeleton covered in a tough, flexible skin and have the ability to regenerate—to grow a new body part to replace a lost or damaged one. A starfish that loses an arm will take about a year to grow a new one. Meanwhile, if the lost arm is still attached to a small part of the central body, it can grow into an entirely new starfish!

💡 *Know it all!*

● The woodlouse is the only crustacean to live on land.

● Starfish have two stomachs. Some starfish can push one of their stomachs outside their body to surround their prey and pull it inside.

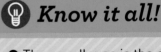

Worms, Mollusks, and Arachnids

Here are three animal groups you might find right outside your house! They live in most parts of the world.

The biggest snail is the giant snail, found in parts of tropical Africa. It grows up to 12 inches (30 cm) long.

If an earthworm is accidentally cut in half, only one half will survive—the half with the fatter center part called the saddle.

Saddle

Some spiders weave webs and then wait for prey to fly into the sticky threads.

Worms

Worms live in all kinds of habitats, from soil to the insides of animal bodies. Some species are many feet long, while others are so small they can be seen only with a microscope. Earthworms are segmented, which means their bodies are made up of sections. They eat their own weight in soil each day and push the same amount out as waste, helping to break up the soil and enrich it.

Mollusks

Mollusks are soft-bodied invertebrates. Some of them grow hard shells. They include snails, slugs, octopuses, squid, and shellfish. Snails and slugs produce slime under the front of their bodies, which they can then glide over. As snails grow they gradually enlarge their shells by oozing a slimy liquid that hardens, adding new layers to the shell's coiled spiral.

Arachnids

There are around thirty-seven thousand species of arachnids, including spiders, scorpions, and ticks. They are invertebrates and have four pairs of jointed legs. Some spiders use their front legs rather like arms for grabbing prey. Most spiders have poisonous fangs, which they use to inject poison to paralyze or kill their victims. Spiders produce silk threads, which they use to spin webs or to weave tiny sacs to protect their eggs.

Hot shots!

★ **ARE YOU LOOKING AT ME?**

This wolf spider looks as if it has two eyes, but in fact it has eight. It pounces on its prey rather than trapping food in a web.

Where in the world?

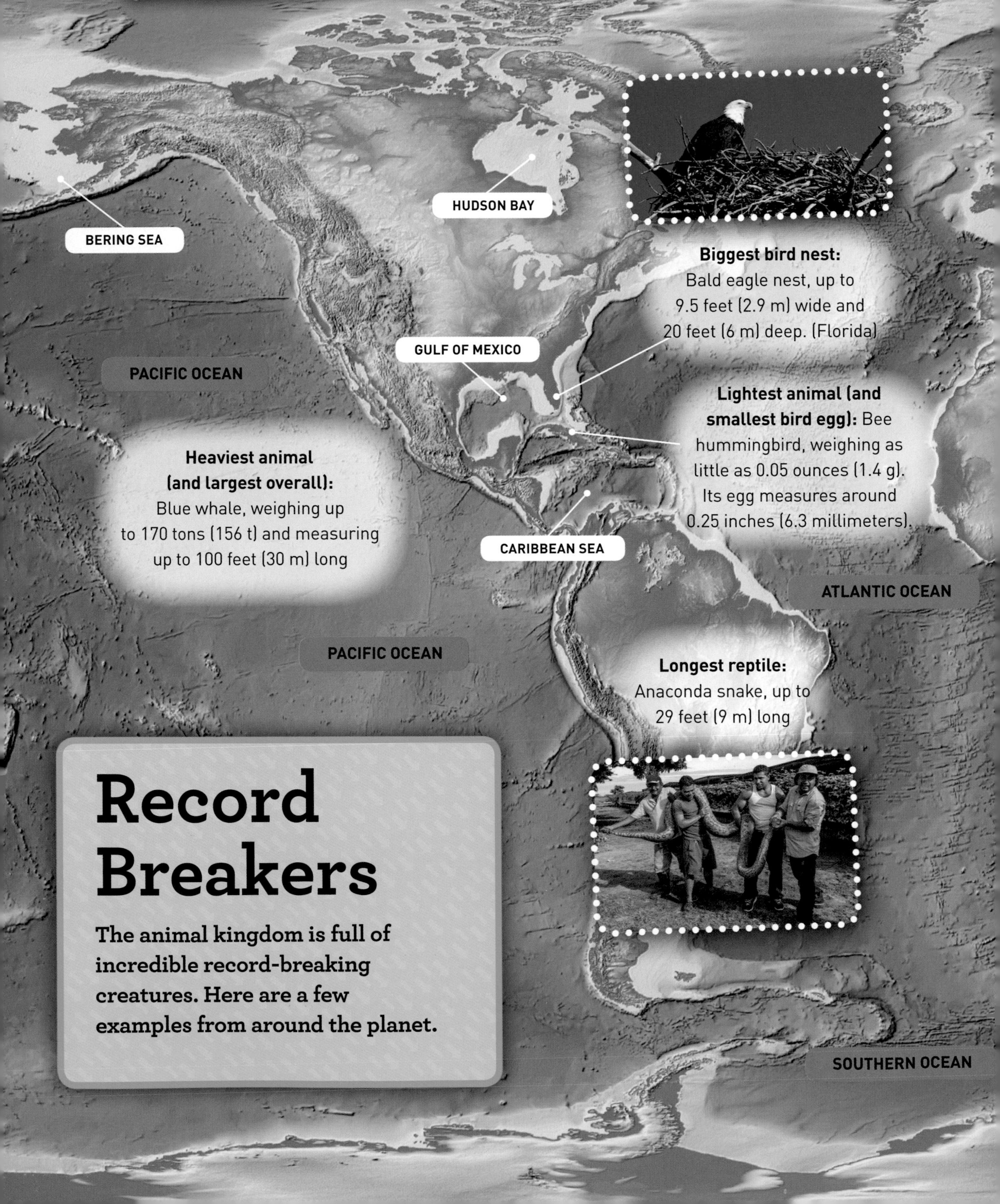

HUDSON BAY

BERING SEA

Biggest bird nest:
Bald eagle nest, up to
9.5 feet (2.9 m) wide and
20 feet (6 m) deep. (Florida)

GULF OF MEXICO

PACIFIC OCEAN

**Lightest animal (and
smallest bird egg):** Bee
hummingbird, weighing as
little as 0.05 ounces (1.4 g).
Its egg measures around
0.25 inches (6.3 millimeters).

**Heaviest animal
(and largest overall):**
Blue whale, weighing up
to 170 tons (156 t) and measuring
up to 100 feet (30 m) long

CARIBBEAN SEA

ATLANTIC OCEAN

PACIFIC OCEAN

Longest reptile:
Anaconda snake, up to
29 feet (9 m) long

Record Breakers

The animal kingdom is full of
incredible record-breaking
creatures. Here are a few
examples from around the planet.

SOUTHERN OCEAN

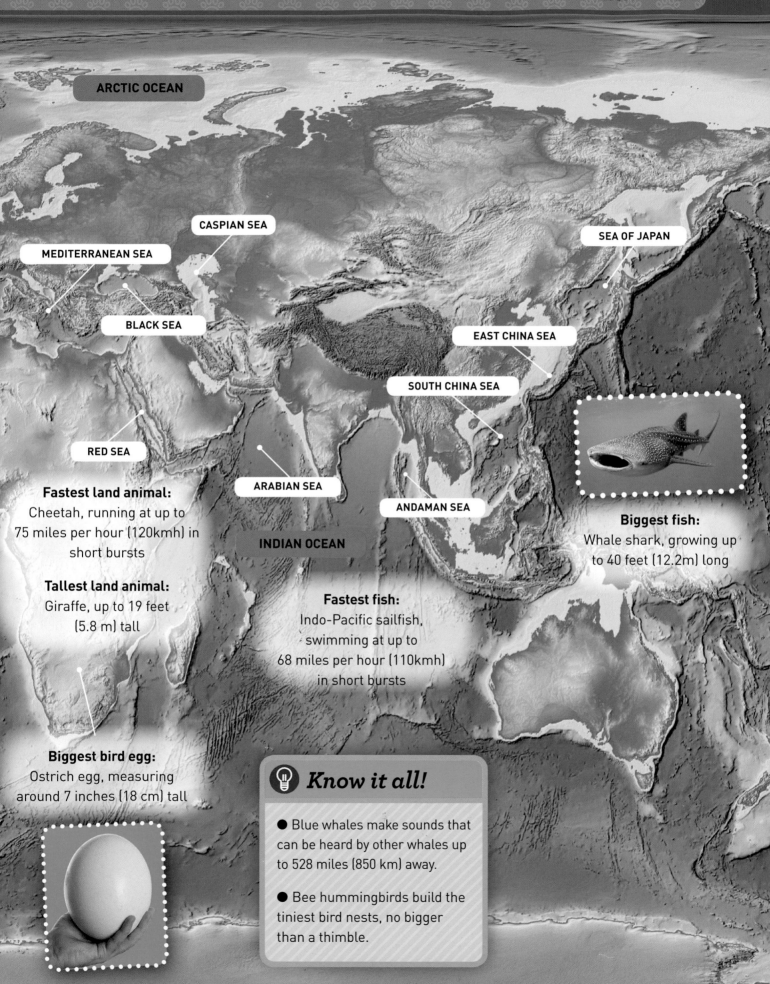

ARCTIC OCEAN

CASPIAN SEA

SEA OF JAPAN

MEDITERRANEAN SEA

BLACK SEA

EAST CHINA SEA

SOUTH CHINA SEA

RED SEA

ARABIAN SEA

ANDAMAN SEA

Biggest fish:
Whale shark, growing up
to 40 feet (12.2m) long

Fastest land animal:
Cheetah, running at up to
75 miles per hour (120kmh) in
short bursts

INDIAN OCEAN

Tallest land animal:
Giraffe, up to 19 feet
(5.8 m) tall

Fastest fish:
Indo-Pacific sailfish,
swimming at up to
68 miles per hour (110kmh)
in short bursts

Biggest bird egg:
Ostrich egg, measuring
around 7 inches (18 cm) tall

Know it all!

● Blue whales make sounds that
can be heard by other whales up
to 528 miles (850 km) away.

● Bee hummingbirds build the
tiniest bird nests, no bigger
than a thimble.

🐾 Animal builders

Animals build permanent dens, temporary nests, and burrows to keep themselves and their young safe.

Den Builders

Beavers are the best animal den builders. They gnaw through tree trunks and use the logs to build dams across streams. A dam holds back water to make a deep pool where the beavers build their home, called a lodge. The lodge has handy underwater entrances and a cozy, dry inside room with a floor of soft, finely grated wood.

A field mouse with its tiny babies, protected in a hidden burrow

A beaver dam holds back water, creating a deep pool behind it.

Insect builders

The best insect builders are African termites. Millions of them work together to build nests called termitariums, which can be up to 26 feet (8 m) tall. Each termite chews earth mixed with spit to make tiny pellets to add to the nest wall. The pellets dry hard, eventually building up to provide a cool shelter for up to two million termites. Underground tunnels are the only way in and out, and chimneys rise up through the middle of the nest, helping to keep it comfortably cool and aired.

A termite mound in Africa. Millions of tiny termites live inside.

Burrow Diggers

Many animals dig burrows to give themselves shelter and safety. The burrow diggers often have special body parts to help them in their work. For instance, moles and armadillos both have big spade-like front feet. Rabbits dig especially large burrows called warrens. Large warrens have been known to have more than two thousand different entrances.

💡 Know it all!

● Beavers live in families of up to twelve. A family of beavers would take about a week to build a dam 33 feet (10 m) long.

● Beavers have strong jaws and teeth with twice the chewing power of humans.

● In every termite nest there is a queen and at least one king. They stay in a "royal chamber" where they are fed and cared for by worker termites.

Animal babies

All animal species must breed to survive. Most animals give birth to young at certain times of the year, when there is plenty of food for them to eat.

A gorilla infant clings to its mother.

The best parents

Most types of fish, insects, amphibians, and reptiles lay their eggs and then abandon them. Birds and mammals tend to look after their young, protecting them and teaching them life skills. For instance, most monkey mothers carry their babies with them as they grow, teaching them where to find food.

Hero dad

Penguins breed in freezing Antarctica. Most give birth in spring, but not the emperor penguin. The female lays an egg and then swims away to feed in the ocean, leaving the male to balance the egg on his feet and keep it warm under a pouch of skin through winter. The males huddle together for around sixty-four days, through freezing darkness and snow blizzards. The female returns as the chick hatches.

An emperor penguin father and chick, having survived a tough winter.

Both mom and dad

Most animals are either male or female, but some creatures are not. The very simplest creatures—amoebae—are made up of just one cell that reproduces by splitting in half to form two. Some simple animals such as sea corals make new creatures by budding. They grow a small branch that eventually splits off to become a new coral.

A simple underwater creature called a hydra budding (making mini versions of itself)

Camouflage and Color

Some animals have camouflage patterns on their skin to help them hide in their surroundings. This keeps them hidden from enemies or helps them to creep up unseen on other creatures.

A sea dragon has skin extensions that make it look like a seaweed leaf.

Hard to spot

Camouflaged animals are hard to see against their surroundings. For example, a flatfish such as a plaice has a speckled skin that makes it hard to see among the sand and pebbles of the seabed. Young deer have spotted markings that make them hard to locate in the dappled light of a forest. The deer needs protection from predators, but the flatfish is likely to be hiding, waiting for prey to swim by.

A young deer is hard to spot on the forest floor because of its skin markings.

Brilliant body shapes

An animal's body shape can help to hide it successfully. For instance, a stick insect is hard to spot on a branch. A leaf insect is green and leaf-shaped, and the sea dragon, a type of seahorse, has skin extensions that make it look like a piece of frilly seaweed.

This octopus is changing color, perhaps to match its surroundings.

Changing color

Some creatures can change color to match their surroundings or sometimes to signal their mood to other animals of the same species. They can alter their markings due to special color cells, called chromatophores, in their skin. Signals from the animal's brain make the cells smaller or larger, varying the skin color. Squid, octopuses, and chameleons all have this ability.

💡 Know it all!

● A chameleon's color alters with its mood. The calmer it feels, the paler its skin. A dark red chameleon is angry.

● Some Arctic animals turn white in winter so they are camouflaged against the snow. Arctic foxes, ptarmigans, and snowshoe rabbits all adapt their colors for winter.

🐾 Deadly Poison

Lots of creatures produce poison, either to kill other animals or to warn enemies not to eat them.

Poisonous tails

Animals such as stingrays and scorpions use poisonous tail stings as defense. The stingray has a sharp, poison-coated spike on its tail, which it uses as a weapon if it feels threatened. Scorpions have defensive stings on their tails, which curl up when they feel threatened. Most scorpion stings are relatively harmless to humans, but the African deathstalker scorpion can cause death with its powerful venom.

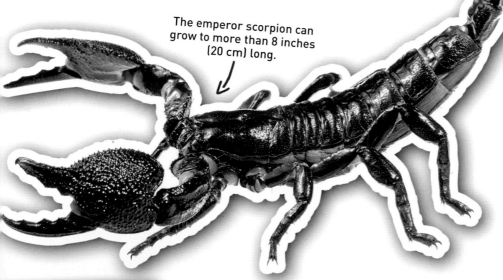

The emperor scorpion can grow to more than 8 inches (20 cm) long.

💡 Know it all!

● The hooded pitohui bird, found in New Guinea, is a rare example of a poisonous bird. Its skin and feathers contain powerful poison.

● There are two poisonous mammals. The male duck-billed platypus has poisonous spurs (spikes) on its back legs. The slow loris makes a poison on the inside of its elbows, which it wipes on its babies to protect them from predators.

Poisonous skin

The tiny South American poison dart frog is the most poisonous animal on Earth. If it is threatened with attack, it sweats its super-deadly poison out through its skin. The frog makes the poison in its body from chemicals found in the ants that it eats in the rain forest. When kept in zoos and fed different food, it is no longer harmful. Indigenous South Americans use the frog poison to tip their hunting darts.

When a snake strikes it produces venom.

The inland taipan, the world's most venomous land snake

Poisonous fangs

Some snakes have venomous fangs. When they bite, venom runs down grooves in the fangs. The world's most venomous land snake is the inland taipan of Australia, but luckily it is shy and rarely bites. Sea snakes are even more venomous. For example, the beaked sea snake's venom is up to eight times stronger than a cobra's venom. Sea snakes are found in the Indian and western Pacific Oceans.

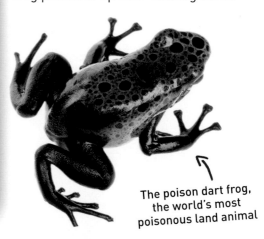

The poison dart frog, the world's most poisonous land animal

🐾 Hibernation

Some animals hibernate, which means they go into a deep sleep through the cold winter. They do this when food becomes scarce and they need to save energy.

A squirrel gets ready for winter by gathering food.

Hibernating bats

During hibernation

During hibernation the body slows itself down. Here's what happens:

- The body's temperature drops.
- The heartbeat slows, using less energy but keeping the animal alive.
- Breathing slows.
- The body uses its fat reserves as food.

Getting ready

Before hibernation, animals will eat as much as they can to fatten themselves. Then they will find a safe place to rest. A mammal such as a black bear or a bat might find a cave. Rodents such as squirrels or mice might settle in a hole in a tree. Hibernating frogs and toads might burrow underground, and some fish hibernate by floating motionless near the bottom of a lake.

Asleep for weeks

Animals hibernate for different amounts of time. Some hibernators might occasionally wake up and go outside, warming themselves by moving around, before going back to sleep. Female bears and polar bears give birth to their cubs in hidden dens during this time. Finally, when spring returns, the hibernators come outside to look for food again.

Baby polar bears come out of their den, after a winter hidden away with their mother.

💡 Know it all!

- During hibernation, a black bear's heartbeat can go down from fifty beats to eight beats per minute.

- Some hibernating bats breathe as little as once every two hours.

- Alpine marmots hibernate for up to eight months a year.

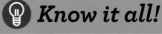

Animal Communication

Animals communicate with each other in many different ways. They might want to warn each other of danger or just make contact with other animals.

A howler monkey calls loudly in the treetops.

Dogs smell each other when they meet.

A wolf communicates aggression by lowering its ears and showing its teeth.

Using noise

The noisiest land animal calls come from the South American howler monkey, which screeches from its perch up in the rain forest trees to communicate with other monkeys in its group. Its screech is amplified (made louder) by a piece of throat skin that inflates and acts like a voice box, sending the call 2.5 to 3 miles (4 to 5 km) away. The noisiest animal of all is the blue whale, whose underwater whistling sound is louder than a jet plane.

Using smell

Many animals communicate using smell. They might mark out their territory with smelly urine or dung, so that rival animals will stay away. They may use scent to attract a mate, too. For instance, some male moths can detect the scent of a female moth up to 2.5 miles (4 km) away. Some animals have special scent glands for producing smells. A dog's scent glands are in its backside, which is why other dogs sniff each other from behind.

Using sight

Animals sometimes communicate with each other using body language. Pack animals such as dogs and wolves do this. A dog that meets a more important dog will put its tail down between its legs to show that it is no threat, for example. A dog signals happiness by wagging its tail, and it shows aggression by baring its teeth. Other dogs will recognize these body signals and understand what they mean.

Endangered Animals

Endangered animals are creatures that are in danger of dying out because there are so few of them left to breed. The way that humans have changed the planet has greatly increased the number of endangered animal species.

Hunted down

In the past, many whales were hunted for their blubber (fat) and other body products, until some whales became very rare. For instance, in 1930 there were more than 200,000 blue whales, but they were hunted until their numbers dropped to around 2,000. Now whale hunting is limited by international law, and the number of blue whales is going up once again. There are now thought to be around 4,500.

The sperm whale was once hunted for the oil stored in its head. Now its hunting is restricted and its numbers are growing again.

Stolen or killed

Rare creatures are valuable, so they risk being captured and illegally sold to smugglers. There are laws against animal smuggling and also against hunting rare animals for their body parts.

When rain forests are destroyed animals lose their homes.

Losing a home

Animals numbers fall when their homes are destroyed. For instance, vast areas of rain forest are now being cut down for logging or for farmland, leading to many more species of animals and plants being put on the endangered list. Changes in the world's climate are leading to loss of habitat, too. For instance, in the Arctic, polar bears are finding it hard to survive as the polar ice cap grows smaller.

Many sea turtle species are now rare, and hunting them is restricted.

Hot shots!

⭐ COMING BACK?

Golden lion tamarin monkeys from the South American rain forest were in danger of dying out as their habitat is being destroyed—but their numbers are now creeping up, thanks to conservation work.

Extinct Animals

An extinct species is one that has completely died out. It is estimated that around twenty thousand animal and plant species become extinct each year, but the number may well be far higher.

Bye, bye birds

The dodo bird is one of the world's most famous extinct animals. It was a peaceful, flightless bird that once lived on the island of Mauritius, but it was quickly killed off in the seventeenth century when humans arrived on the island and ate the birds. The biggest bird ever, the elephant bird also died out on Mauritius in the seventeenth century. It grew to more than 10 feet (3 m) tall and had eggs 13 inches (34 cm) long.

A drawing of the dodo bird, which became extinct in the seventeenth century

Facts & figures

Here is a list of species on the verge of extinction during the writing of this book. Some may be extinct by the time you read this:

Javan rhino (Indonesia): Fewer than sixty left

Golden-headed lemur (Vietnam): Fewer than seventy left

Vaquita (small whale from Gulf of California): two hundred to three hundred left

Cross river gorilla (Nigeria, Cameroon): Fewer than three hundred left

Sumatran tiger (Indonesia): Fewer than six hundred left

Black-footed ferret (North America): About one thousand left

Borneo pygmy elephant: About fifteen hundred left

Giant panda (Asia): About two thousand left

Today's extinctions

More and more animals are becoming extinct. It is thought that one in four mammal species, one in eight bird species, and one in three amphibian species are now in danger of dying out.

Sumatran tigers are one of the mammal species facing extinction.

Back from the dead

Occasionally an animal is declared extinct and then found again. The coelacanth fish was thought to have died out seventy million years ago, but then one was found alive in 1978. In 2012, a little Mediterranean oil beetle was discovered on an English clifftop, which surprised beetle experts who had thought it was extinct.

A coelacanth, rediscovered in 1978

Saving Animals

All over the world people are working to protect animals from harm and to save them from extinction.

Critically endangered black rhinos have been relocated to safer homes.

Wildlife reserves

Reserves are areas of land set aside to provide safe homes for rare creatures, where they can escape hunting or habitat destruction. Conservationists monitor the animals there to see how well they are surviving. For instance, tigers in reserves across India and Asia are tracked to try to ensure their safety.

Moving to a new home

Sometimes threatened wild animals are "translocated," which means they are captured and moved to a new, safer home. Rhinos have been moved to safe reserves in Africa this way. The rhinos are darted with a tranquilizer, which puts them to sleep. Sometimes they are winched in a net by helicopter and flown to their new location.

Wildlife parks

Sometimes rare creatures are kept in zoos and wildlife parks where they can safely breed. Then the animals are released back into the wild to build up the species' numbers. It takes a lot of planning and careful study of the animals to successfully "rewild" them. The US has rewilded a few of its endangered species, including the lynx in Colorado, the giant condor in California, and the black-footed ferret on the Great Plains.

The lynx has been reintroduced in Colorado.

Hot shots!

UNDERSEA SAFETY

Marine reserves such as this one in the Red Sea, Egypt, have been set up around the world, the underwater equivalent of a wildlife reserve on land. Here sea creatures such as delicate corals can be protected.

Saving Animals with Science

Conservationists are using the latest scientific methods to try to save endangered species and may even be able to reintroduce extinct species one day.

The first-ever cloned animal was Dolly the sheep. She turned out to have health problems, however.

Scientists extract DNA from animal cells and analyze it to create a DNA map of animal populations.

A scientist at work at a Frozen Ark facility, where frozen animal DNA is preserved and stored

Animal cloning

Cloning is a way of producing an animal that is a copy of another creature. It is done by making identical copies of existing cells in a laboratory. These may eventually become a baby creature. Scientists have cloned farm animals and are working to clone endangered species, too. It is possible that tigers and pandas might one day be saved by cloning, but it is not easy or certain.

The Frozen Ark

The Frozen Ark is a project to store the DNA of endangered animals. DNA is the coded information inside an animal's cells—information that triggers how the body grows and behaves. In each Frozen Ark facility around the world, frozen animal DNA is stored, preserving it so that, in the future, scientists will be able to study it and may even be able to use it for cloning.

DNA mapping

Scientists sometimes tranquilize endangered wild animals to take DNA samples from them. The scientists can work out from the samples which animals are related to each other. Using the DNA information, they can see how widely animal populations are spread and decide if they need help to survive.

Glossary

Amphibians A group of animals that live partly in water and partly on land.

Arachnids The group of animals that contains spiders.

Carnivore An animal that eats only meat.

Cartilaginous Fish that have skeletons made of tough, gristly material called cartilage, instead of bone.

Chromatophores Cells in the skin of some animals that can get smaller or larger to change the skin's color.

Cloning A way of producing an animal that is an exact copy of another animal.

Crustaceans A group of animals with hard shells. Lobsters and crabs are crustaceans.

DNA Coded information inside every animal cell that controls how the body grows and behaves.

Echinoderms A group of animals that live mainly underwater and have endoskeletons covered with a tough, flexible skin. Sea urchins and sea stars are echinoderms.

Ecosystem A community of plants and animals in a particular environment.

Exoskeleton A protective skeleton on the outside of the body.

Extinction When an animal species completely dies out.

Genus A grouping of animals that are alike. For instance, different types of cat are all in the genus *Felidae* (Latin for "cats").

Gills Feather-like organs behind the head, through which water passes and oxygen is taken up.

Herbivore An animal that eats only plants.

Hibernation An extended sleep that some animals have during winter, to save energy.

Indigenous Originating or starting in a particular place; native.

Omnivore An animal that eats both meat and plants.

Phylum A large grouping of animals.

Primate A grouping of mammals that includes monkeys, lemurs, apes, and humans.

Pupa A stage in an insect's growth when it hides inside a hard case and changes into an adult.

Reptiles A group of animals that are cold blooded and have scaly, waterproof skin.

Rewilding Reintroducing animals into the wild from zoos and wildlife parks.

Segmented Made up of sections.

Species The name of a particular type of animal that is unique and is capable of interbreeding.

Swim bladder An air-filled sac inside a fish's body, which helps the fish to float.

Taxonomy The classification (organizing and naming) of animals into groups.

Translocation The capturing and moving of wild animals to a new, safer home in the wild.

Venom Poison put by one animal into another animal, through biting, stinging, or piercing it.

Vertebrate An animal with a backbone.

Zoology The study of animals.

Further Information

BOOKS

Burnie, David, and Don E. Wilson. *Animal: The Definitive Visual Guide*. Revised Updated Edition. New York: DK, 2011.

Otfinoski, Steven. *Zookeeper*. Careers with Animals. New York: Cavendish Square Publishing, 2014.

Spelman, Lucy. *National Geographic Animal Encyclopedia: 2,500 Animals with Photos, Maps, and More*. Des Moines, IA: National Geographic Children's Books, 2012.

Stefoff, Rebecca. *How Animals Think*. Animal Behavior Revealed. New York: Cavendish Square Publishing, 2013.

WEBSITES

Animal Planet Wild Animals

www.animalplanet.com/wild-animals/

Watch videos on fish, mammals, monsters, and human interaction, and read articles created by Discovery Communications.

National Geographic Animals

animals.nationalgeographic.com/animals/

Explore the world of animals through stories, videos, and photos from one of the leaders in information about our world.

Index

Page numbers in **boldface** are illustrations. Entries in **boldface** are glossary terms.

Billywise

Judith Nicholls

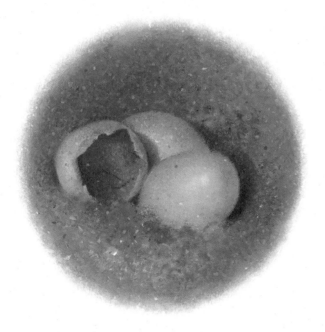

illustrated by
Jason Cockcroft

BLOOMSBURY
CHILDREN'S
BOOKS

From a mole-black hole
in the oldest oak,
deep in the heart
of the fern-brushed wood …

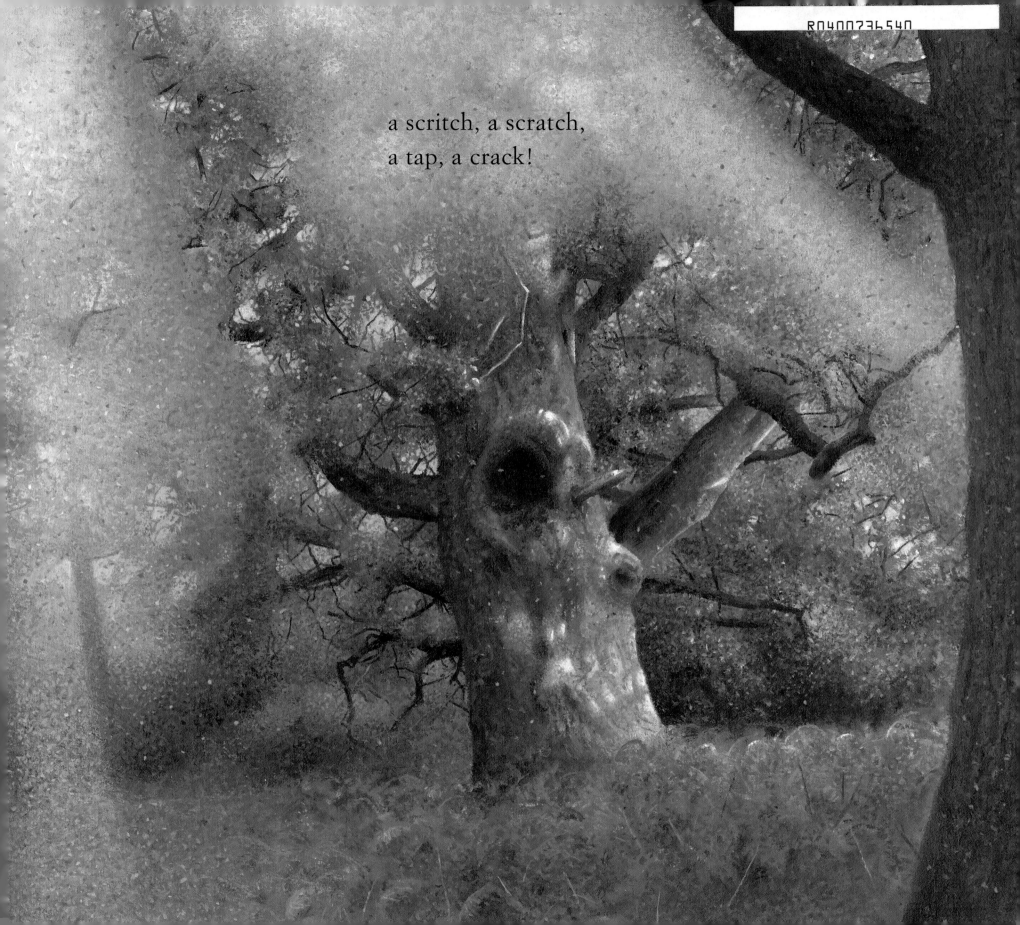

a scritch, a scratch,
a tap, a crack!

A pale egg split …
and Billywise crept out of it.

'Who are *you*?' murmured moth
from the shadowy glade.
'You're not rough,
you're not tough,
just a small ball of fluff ...
you wouldn't make *anyone* afraid!'

'Who am I?' whispered Billywise,
safe in his shady nest.
But his mother, fondly feeding him, said,
'*Hush*! Just eat and rest!'

'You will grow, you will prowl,
you will slide through the air;
you will swoop, loop-the-loop,
you will stare, you will glare ...
as silently as moonlight
you'll glide through the midnight air.'

But Billywise just blinked in fear
and whispered,
'I won't dare!'

Next night,
whilst his mother searched for food …

'Who are *you*?' squeaked squirrel,
peering from a branch nearby.
'You can't catch me,
I'd beat you on any tree –
and it doesn't look as if *you'll* ever fly!'

'Who am I?' whispered Billywise,
huddling in his nest.
But his mother, fondly feeding him, said,
'*Hush*! Just eat and rest!'

'You will grow, you will prowl,
you will slide through the air;
you will swoop, loop-the-loop,
you will stare, you will glare …
as silently as moonlight
you'll glide through the midnight air.'

But Billywise just blinked in fear
and whispered,
'I won't dare!'

Before long there were three
in the oldest oak:
Billywise, Jennyhowlett and Pudge.

And they *grew*.

Billywise cried, '*Please*,
why are those two there?
Do I *have* to share?
This really *is* a squash and a squeeze!'

They pushed and wriggled,
they squeezed and wiggled
until, at last, they slept.

They slept all day,
then watched their mother fly away
as the sunlight stole from the wood …

And they grew!
They grew and they GREW,
and soon Billywise
dreamt of *space*.

He longed to swoop,
loop-the-loop,
to slide through the air,
as silently as moonlight
to glide through the midnight air.

But …
did he dare?

One night,
when the moon was high overhead,
Billywise stepped up to the edge of the nest,
with searching eyes and wings outspread.

And his mother said,

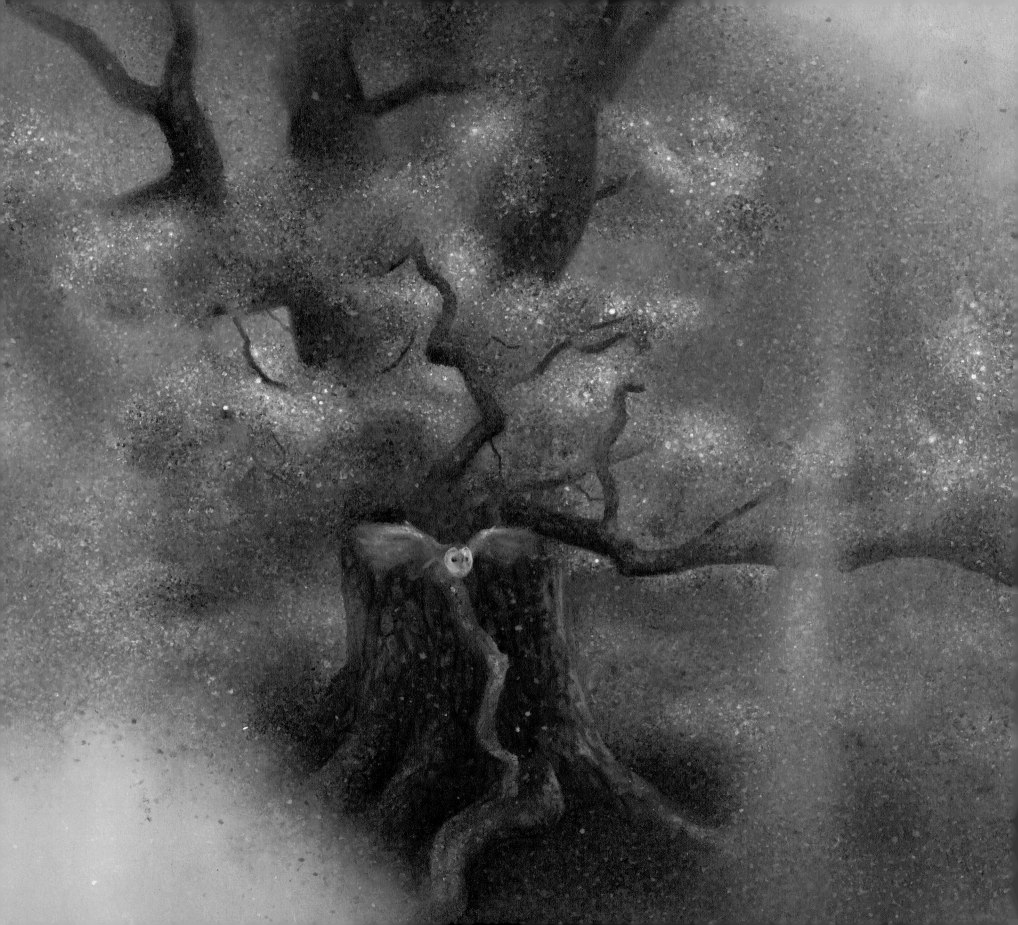

'If you tried,
you could glide!

Spread your wings to the side,
fix your ears on the night,
let the stars light your flight
and aim for the moon!'

'You're an OWL, Billywise!
You can dive, you can prowl,
you can slide through the air;
you can swoop, loop-the-loop,
you can stare, you can glare!'

'JUMP, Billywise!

As silently as moonlight,
glide through that midnight air!'

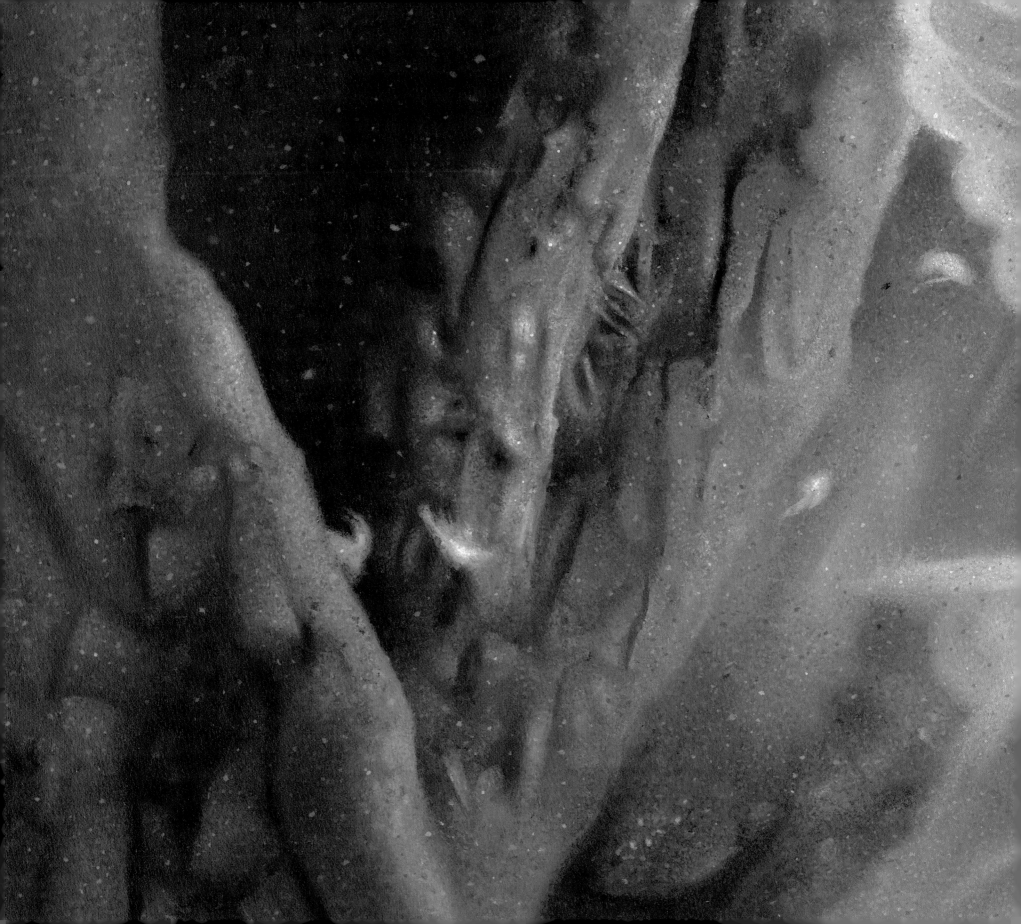

Billywise breathed deeply,
spread his wings to the watching wood
and cried,

'I'm an *owl*,
I dare, I dare!'